Think on
These Things

Think on These Things

Doreen Irvine

Marshall Pickering

Marshall Morgan and Scott
Marshall Pickering
3 Beggarwood Lane, Basingstoke, Hants RG23 7LP, UK

Copyright © 1988 Doreen Irvine
First published in 1988 by Marshall Morgan and Scott
Publications Ltd
Part of the Marshall Pickering Holdings Group
A subsidiary of the Zondervan Corporation

British Library CIP Data

Irvine, Doreen
  Think on these things: reflections for all seasons in poetry and
  prose.
  1. Devotional literature
  I. Title
  242   BV4832.2

  ISBN: 0-551-01594 2

Text set in Century Textbook by Brian Robinson, Buckingham
Printed in Great Britain by Richard Clay Ltd, Bungay, Suffolk

Contents

Introduction

I have been writing poetry now for some years, and have had the joy of seeing some of them published in Christian magazines, and sent all over the world to those working on the mission field. I have received many letters telling me how they have been blessed and encouraged by them. I have been asked, 'Why don't you put your poems into a book?' Well, now I have just done that, and I pray that they will bring much joy, blessing, and comfort to those who read them.

Every December people wish each other a 'Merry Christmas and a happy New Year.' Complete strangers smile at each other and exchange this greeting. It must have been repeated many thousands of times all over the world. What a pity it cannot be like that all the year round. God wants it to be like that. 'Peace on earth and goodwill to men' all the time.

I have heard so many people say at the end of the old year, 'It's been a bad year for me.' Things have happened to them that have brought much sadness and pain, and they are very glad the old year is over, and hope for better things in the year ahead. For Christians it is different. Whatever the season, whatever the future holds, sadness or sunshine, joy or pain, they know that their times are in the hands of their heavenly Father and that they will be safe—He will be with them in every situation and help them in their time of need. Christians can look back over the old year with thankful, grateful hearts. The Master has helped them in the day of trouble, and they can trust Him for the future.

If only the unbelievers would put their trust in the unfailing Saviour, it would not just be a happy New Year, but a *happy new life*! Thinking of the traditional New Year greeting prompted me to write the final poem in this book. I pray that all the poems will be a blessing and encouragement to every believer, and a challenge to unbelievers to put their trust in the unfailing Saviour, not only now, but in the days ahead, should the Lord tarry.

Doreen Irvine

Spring

As many people know through my testimony, and my book, *From Witchcraft to Christ*, I was once a prostitute, drug addict and witch. It was a life full of disappointments, and utter loneliness. I looked for love, as a child, as an adult, but I searched in vain, I searched in the wrong places, and all I found was a low, degrading type of love, which was not love at all. It did not lift me up, it dragged me down to the depths of deep despair and misery.

I can relate to prostitutes, I know how many of them feel, always looking for that special someone who would really care about them—someone kind, and gentle, someone different, someone good—just as I did once. Imagine my joy when I found that someone—the Lord Jesus Christ. He changed me completely, washing away the shame of prostitution, filling my life with His light and love. He was unlike any man I had ever met before. He is the Son of God, and the Son of man. He loved me even in my sin and shame, and lifted me up from the pit of dark despair. He delivered me from all the evil powers of darkness that had possessed me and controlled me for so many long years. He set me free—what a Saviour!

Although I can still remember the dark lonely streets of London, the utter emptiness inside that brought me so much pain, the memory does not haunt me any more. He bound up the wounds that transgression had made, and the scars are healed. I can speak freely, without any fear, and I am able to witness to many who are in the same dark bondage that I was in, telling them of my past experiences, telling them how the living Saviour set me free from it all, telling them that what He has done for me He can do for them. It has been such a tremendous joy to lead some of them to Jesus Christ.

There is even more prostitution today in our major cities. More and more young women are turning to this kind of life, and sad to say, the great problem of unemployment is adding to their numbers. Young people want life, they want money, and prostitution still pays well in terms of easy cash. But money cannot buy happiness, as I and many others have found out. The price you have to pay in terms of health, peace, and happiness in mind, soul and spirit, is far higher. There is a way out of it all, through the salvation of Jesus Christ, and I believe He is the *only* way out. He can reach anyone, no matter how low they have sunk. He lifted me up, and He can lift them up also.

Let me take you on an imaginary journey down a London slum, and tell you a story in verse. This story is not a true one, but it could happen. We are still living in the day of God's grace, and miracles still happen today. One happened to me!

Conversion in London Slum

In a London slum one dark and dismal night,
The lamps along a gloomy street, threw out a dim and
    mellow light,
Few passers-by remained where many had been,
Now they were hastily retreating from the scene,
Some to homes alight with love, and joy, and peace,
With eager hurrying footsteps made their way,
Whilst others homeless, and friendless, sought increase
In pleasure's palaces, and bent on worldly fame their
    interests lay.

But wait! there's one who's lingering in the shadows there,
Her face, her form, spell misery, dark woe, and deep
    despair,
For all her life was spent, in darkest sin and shame,
For all the pleasures she had tasted were in vain,
Now with the mind of one determined in her misery to
    drown,
Not waiting now for questions or delays,
Not noticing a crowd of happy people gathering round,
Made haste towards the riverside, the parapet, and quays.

'Today if you would hear this voice, Oh harden not your
    heart,
Jesus is waiting outside the door, His pardon and peace to
    impart.'
The heavenly message rang forth loud and clear,
Perchance the words may reach some drooping sinners ear,
'Oh happy rest, sweet, happy rest, Jesus will give you
    rest,'
A voice was sweetly singing soft and low,
'Friend of the friendless, hope of all hopelessness
He alone can wash your sin stains, whiter than the driven
    snow.'

Then—like a sudden shaft of sunlight after a stormy sky,
Hope came dawning o'er her spirit and slowly she ventured
nigh
She could bear the suspense no longer, and cried with a
fervent cry,
'Sir, tell me plainly can he care for such a poor wretch as I?'
The answer came sure and swiftly, like balm on her sin-sick
soul—
'He came not to call the righteous but for sinners to repent,
Yes, Jesus cares and longs to wash and make you fully
whole,
So come now to the Blessed Redeemer—Come e'er the day
be spent.'

And if you had been there at that scene that night,
You would have seen that gloomy street ablaze with
heavenly light.
As with soul so repentant, for long wasted years
She told all to the Saviour, and spared not her tears,
Among that band of happy people, now that saint is often
stood,
Telling out the grand old story, to the lonely lost in sin,
In that darkest London slum, tells them of a cross of wood,
Where once Jesus died to save them, gave His life their
souls to win.

I stood behind a wall for many long, dark, empty years—sad, alone, reflective, weighed down with many heavy cares. Here I was unguarded from the enemy of souls, unprotected from the imaginings of my mind, from the hauntings of the past, unhappy, yes, tragic events in my life. The unknown future lurked, threatening, in the gloomy shadows. It was a wall of fear so huge, so black, so stark in its reality, it was insurmountable. It was a wall of sin and shame that separated me from God and everything that was good, pure and upright.

Now that wall has been removed, broken down, I stand complete in Him, unblemished and confident of His accepting love, guarded by His constant presence. I know He is with me. The shameful past is behind, forgiven and healed, and my future is secure in Him.

But it is possible for other walls to be built. Even Christians can build up barriers and walls. A wall of doubt and uncertainty can block the Christian pathway and bring other walls of confusion and pain. A wall of fear can bring total darkness to the soul. You can build up a wall of resentment, anger and distrust that cuts off all blessing and peace. You can build up a wall to protect yourself from the hurts of life that will keep you shut away, imprisoned within yourself, where you are unable to communicate with anyone at all. Building up a wall to keep hurts out only keeps hurts in.

Life, even for the Christian, brings many hurtful happenings and trying experiences. How we react to them either enriches us or embitters us. To respond with sensitivity and grace will create an environment that helps mend broken hearts and the fragmented, shattered relationships of lost, desperate people all around us. It is only as we suffer from our own lack of virtue, and know times of failure, trials and testings, that we are able to refresh and refill others who suffer.

When I show real understanding, real compassionate love, I am able to see why I myself walked those deep, dark, desperate valleys. Those trying pain-filled days and lonely sleepless nights have taught me truths and ideals that can minister to lives. So I must come out from behind the walls that block my Christian pathway, so that I can relate to others, share my experiences, and make myself available. I must forget about my own pain when I see pain in someone else's eyes, forget my own burdens when I see someone else's troubled face, shattered dreams, battered, bruised and broken life.

If I do this, I will look around again afterwards and see the stones of unbelief and doubt, that held my wall together, all lying in a heap upon the ground. The bricks and rubble that made up my wall, that kept me from reaching out to the people in my world—from sunlight, acceptance, fulfilment and love—will lie broken and useless in the dust. There are no walls; they are gone, and I am free!

May Jesus break down every barrier that would hinder us from living a truly victorious Christian life. May our lives be a reflection of His love and grace.

Broken Down Walls
(Ephesians 2:14)

Once I stood behind a wall, a wall of sin and shame,
The wall was high and ugly, and each brick had a name,
Bricks of hate and anger, bricks of fear and doubt,
Rebellion, pride, and thousands more that shut the sunlight
    out.

Each time I tried to scale it, to rid me of my fears,
More bricks of disappointment, dashed hopes, and bitter
    tears;
The wall closed in around me, and quickly it became,
A prison house, a dungeon, with ball, and lock, and chain.

Then into that dark dungeon this glorious message came,
That Jesus really loved me, and died to bear my shame;
The cruel nails that pierced Him, each thorn that made His
    crown,
Each stripe He bore to save me and break the sin walls
    down.

I cried, 'Dear Lord, forgive me, I give my heart to thee;
Oh wash me, cleanse me, heal me, set this poor prisoner
    free.'
A radiant light from heaven broke through the prison wall,
He snapped the chains and whispered, 'I forgive you all.'

He chased away the darkness, He cast out all my fears,
With His gentle nail-scarred hands, He dried those bitter
    tears.
There is no condemnation, He bought me with His blood,
My sins are gone forever, beneath that crimson flood.

Now different walls surround me, of Holy fire and love,
For Jesus is my fortress, He guards me from above;
He is my sure foundation, my strong chief corner stone,
His light and love will guide me, and lead me safely home.

Just as many thousands of people celebrate Christmas —with all the trimmings, parties, presents, feastings and fun—so they celebrate Easter. Easter eggs, Easter buns, holidays, get-togethers. But when it is all over they just carry on and wait for the next time to celebrate something. The message of Easter means nothing to them.

To me the Easter story is alive all the year round. Every day is an Easter Glory, it speaks to me of the empty tomb, a living, loving, caring Christ who walks with me day by day. The glory of Easter is an every-day experience.

He appeared first to Mary Magdalene. She had been an outcast and a woman of ill reputation, just as I once was, and yet she was the one to whom Jesus Christ first appeared and spoke. How much she loved her Lord; she had been forgiven much, therefore she loved Him much. How glorious that Easter morning was to her when she saw the Lord she loved; she spoke to Him, and He to her—He called her by her name, Mary.

The Easter story is glorious, beautiful, real, and exciting. I cannot forget that wonderful dawning when Christ rose from the tomb, it thrills my very soul. He set me free. He removed the stone from my cold, dark heart, and I live because He lives. He lives in me day by day, so every day to me is an Easter Glory. Every day is brand new life, a resurrection day, and oh, what joy to wake up every morning to this new life in Christ, my risen, glorified Lord!

Mary Magdalene was always near Jesus, she knew Him so well, and yet she did not recognise Him at first. But Mary was not looking for someone alive—she was looking for a dead body. Many people today do not recognise Jesus as the risen Saviour—they still see Him hanging on a cross of wood. But Jesus is alive and glorified. He is just the same today as He was yesterday.

The tomb is empty, the Saviour lives. He is risen with healing in His wings. How thrilling to know this living Saviour and to abide under the shadow of His wings. A dead Christ cannot change anyone. A dead Christ cannot change the life of a prostitute, drug addict and witch—only a risen Saviour could do this. He's done it for me and He can do it for you, if you allow Him to. Then for you too, every day will be an Easter Glory.

The Easter Glory

My heart was like a cold, dark tomb
Filling with darkest sin and deepest gloom;
A great hard stone of unbelief before it lay—
THEN JESUS CAME,
And rolled the stone away!

He broke the heavy chains and set me free,
Bringing me peace and glorious liberty,
Flooding my soul with light and love—
What Heavenly bliss!
ONLY A RISEN SAVIOUR COULD DO THIS.

Now every day this is the Easter Glory—
The grand old Gospel Story;
The story of the Cross where Christ was slain,
The message of the empty tomb—He rose again!

From death redeemed,
To life restored,
my EASTER GLORY this—
The Risen Christ,
My Living Lord!

Mount Calvary

Up upon Mount Calvary,
Lo, the Saviour dies alone,
See His head, His hands, His feet,
Look, His blood for sins atone.

Up upon Mount Calvary,
God's Lamb for sinners slain,
His sacred head bowed down with grief,
To bear our sin and shame.

Up upon Mount Calvary,
See, the darkness now descend,
'Forgive them Father,' was His cry,
Proves Himself the sinners' friend.

Up upon Mount Calvary,
It was for me He died,
It was for me the crown of thorns,
The bleeding, wounded side.

Up upon Mount Calvary,
For me His life He gave,
They nailed Him to a cross of wood,
And laid Him in the grave.

A ray of light and healing,
Now shines from Calvary's brow,
Jesus rose up from the dead,
The grave is empty now.

There's room for all at Calvary,
No one is ever turned away,
The light that's shone through ages past,
Still shines as bright today.

He is Risen

The garden tomb is empty, the stone is rolled away,
'Jesus Christ is risen' hear the angels say.
Banished gloom and shadow, gone is doubt and fear,
Gone is death and darkness, life and light is here;
Even earth rejoices, clothing her for Spring,
Showing forth the splendour of the heavenly King.
Flower in every meadow, blossoms on the tree,
Speak of His undying love, and spotless purity.
Hasten now to greet Him, open up the door,
New life, new love, new joy He gives, and peace for
    evermore.

To some prayer is a one-way affair. They do all the talking, all the asking, and wonder why God is silent. We bring our requests and our problems to Him and expect to receive the answers straight away. We say, 'Lord, give us this, give us that, solve this problem, and that problem', and wonder why we do not receive any answers. It is because we do not allow the Lord to speak to us. We are not still and silent in His presence. We dump our thoughts, needs and empty words on Him, and say 'Amen', and wonder why He is silent.

We recognise the importance of prayer. We know it is directly commanded in God's Word—'Pray without ceasing' the Bible says—yet so many neglect prayer altogether, they only pray in extreme emergency. Some feel guilty about neglected prayer, and periodically resolve to develop a consistent, meaningful prayer life. They often fail. Good intentions are lost in the persistent demands of daily life. To some prayer is awkward, difficult and embarrassing, but this should never be. Prayer is the fulfilment of happiness, the key that can unlock doors, and the only way to a victorious life in Christ. Prayer is a matchless opportunity to change situations, to change people, and to be changed ourselves.

The Bible tells us to ask and we will receive, but the Lord not only wants us to ask, but to thank Him. So many forget to thank the Lord for the everyday things like food, shelter, clothes and loved ones. He gave His life for us, let us thank Him for that. He also wants us to praise Him, to worship Him in prayer, just because He is God and He is love. He loves the praises of His children. He wants us to *wait* upon Him in prayer, to be still and silent in His presence so that He can show us things and speak to our hearts in a still, small voice.

Do not think God is silent because He does not care. God's silence can speak to our need and cause us to pause and think about important things, to learn of Him, and to give us a fresh vision and new light. Don't neglect His silence, it could be His answer for you.

Jesus prayed to His Father at Gethsemane, 'Father let this cup pass from me', and God was silent. Again Jesus prayed, 'Father if this cup may not pass away except I drink it, thy will be done'. The Father answered His Son through His silence—and Jesus went to Calvary and died for you and me. Jesus prayed for us before He died and He is still praying for us now at the right hand of His Father in Heaven. He is making intercession for us all the time.

So let us thank Him for everything He has done for us. Let us praise and worship Him who is worthy to be praised. Let us praise and thank Him for what He is doing today, for changing hearts and lives, and thank Him for what He is going to do. If you have never thanked Him before, why not start today? Why not start now? There is provision for all your needs at the feet of Jesus.

Thank You, Lord

Thank you, Lord, for dying on the cross of Calvary,
I'm so grateful that you suffered there for me,
You bore the crown, the cruel nails, the agony and pain,
To set the captive slave of Satan free.

Thank you, Lord, for rising from the tomb where you were
    laid,
For you rose again that I may also live,
You washed my guilty sin away, and now you live in me,
Thank you Jesus for the new life that you give.

Thank you, Jesus, for opening my eyes so I could see,
For I was blind, and could not see the way,
You showed me the light of all thy wondrous love and
    power,
Thank you, Jesus, for still leading me today.

Thank you, Lord, for opening my ears so I can hear,
Every single little word you want to say,
Words of truth and life, with a voice so pure and sweet,
So help me, Lord, to listen and obey.

Thank you for your faithfulness that never, ever fails,
Thank you, Jesus, for the peace and joy you send,
For guarding me and keeping me with strong and loving
    hands,
Thank you, Lord, for calling me your friend.

Thank you, Lord, for using me to glorify thy name,
Thank you for the gifts that you impart,
For helping me to find the lost and lead them unto thee,
Thank you, Lord, for everything, with all my heart.

Summer

Come with me, dear reader, and let me share with you some of the delights of summer days. Let me share with you beauty that I did not know or experience before I found Christ as my Saviour.

A warm breeze fans my cheeks as I leave the little cottage by the sea, and as I walk I watch the gold streaks in the east brighten until the horizon is filled with the majesty of the rising sun. The birds are singing sweetly, full of joy at the prospect of a beautiful day, and the joyful melody pours forth from the skylark poised with an effortless grace in the blue sky. The sun is the master now and lights up the hillside clothed with golden gorse; the quiet meadow is alive with butterflies that flit from one wild flower to another in search of the sweet nectar.

It is not until we know the Creator that we can fully appreciate all this beauty. Look at the primroses and the carpet of bluebells that seem to chime in the leafy woods. Gardens are full of flowers, flowers of every hue; tall trees, the chestnut, pine and oak, deck the lawns which slant away to catch the summer sun. The trees seem to wave a welcome to me as I pass them. All this beauty was made for me and you. Each blade of grass, each rose, each tree. Beauty is for those who see it; I may not have all those lovely flowers in my garden, but I claim them, God made them for me to enjoy.

At last we have reached the sea, the morning breeze has dropped, I feel the warmth of the sun on my arms. The waves roll lazily up on to the brown sand, and burst into a splash of white foam upon the beach, where little children play happily with their buckets and spades, and brightly coloured balls. Distant ships make their way across the calm waves, and the tall majestic cliffs stretch away on either side. It is as if nature unfolds her splendour and lays it on the altar of mankind.

As we continue our stroll we come upon a tiny rippling brook; the water has washed the stones white, and has a

21

musical ring about it as it wends its way to and fro between its mossy green banks. Beside the brook grows a sycamore tree, and this reminds me of the story of Zacchaeus in the Bible, who in his determination to see the Saviour climbed up into its branches.

Everywhere you look there is beauty, even as the golden light and purple twilight fall, it seems that the whole earth is hushed and still, while nature pauses to give thanks to God. A Hallelujah bursts forth from the depths of my being for the glory and beauty of the sunset. The sun is an orb of rosy, golden light sinking down on the horizon, the sky is streaked with pink, crimson, and soft gold. It all seems a fitting tribute to a departing summer day, a fitting tribute to the Son of God.

God-given Beauty

Oh Lord, how manifold are thy works; the earth is full of thy riches. (Ps. 104:24)

There is beauty all around me, as far as I can see,
The sunset, and the twinkling stars, the streams, the honey bee,
I possess the rugged mountains, I possess the leafy trees,
That wave a hearty welcome with every passing breeze.

I possess the stately hollyhock, and tiny flowers, white and blue,
The roses red, the buttercups, and flowers of every hue;
They may not grow in my garden, but I claim them, they are mine,
Beauty is for those who see it, God-given beauty, so divine.

There is beauty in the robin calling to his timid mate,
And the tiny sparrow singing on the farmyard gate.
I possess all that is beautiful, as far as I can see,
I count myself most privileged, God made them all for me.

There is beauty in the lilies, pure and bright and fair,
There is no earthly glory that can with these compare;
Oh let my heart be like the lilies, pure and white,
Let my feet walk in the sunshine of thy heavenly light.

Lord Jesus be the gracious gardener of my heart,
Tend it, and keep it pure and sweet in every single part,
Never let me forget the lessons I have learned,
That into my whole being, loving Master, thou hast burned.

Why is growth in Christ in so many Christians seldom seen, or very, very slow? Why do so many Christians remain in the dust of defeat when they have no business to be there? So many allow Satan to keep them down, keep them from their rightful inheritance in Christ, when they should be growing in the likeness of Him.

It has been a great joy to lead many to Christ, yet I have had to pray for and counsel more Christians than I have non-Christians making their first-time decision for the Lord. A great many of them have admitted that they have never known what it is like to be free, liberated, and able to live a truly victorious life in Christ. How sad! I have spoken to so many who have never been happy because they are bound by so many things—fear, guilt, worry, doubt, depression, and a long list of bondages that keep them in the same state they were in when they first came to Christ for salvation. They are stunted, they are spiritually crippled, robbed of their rightful inheritance of joy, peace, and love. They are still on the milk, and have never been weaned off it, they are still just babes in Christ.

Many of the problems are deep-rooted, and stem from tragic past events in their lives, for which they have never received inner healing: the wounds remain, so they have never been able to progress in their Christian life, and have never been able to grow up in the full stature of Christ.

When we come to Christ for forgiveness and repent of our sins, this is not the end but rather the beginning of a new way of life—our lives from that moment on should change, and we should go on, progress into righteousness, purity, holiness, and grow daily more and more like the Lord Jesus Christ. But so many stop at the same place, always doing the same things, never able to get the victory over sin, never able to overcome the enemy of souls.

May I say here, firmly but kindly, that I have met some Christians who go to church regularly, listen to the sermons, go through all the motions, but never change. Some are Sunday school teachers, elders, deacons: they look all right outwardly, but inwardly they are still hot-tempered, selfish, jealous, unkind, impure and worldly— they have never grown in the Lord and in His likeness, and

24

some have never been properly taught how to grow in grace and in the knowledge of His Word.

Just as you formed habits that led you to failure and sin and disgrace, and separated you from God and his righteousness, you should begin to form habits that lead you into holiness and the image of Christ. This is His perfect plan for your Christian life. There is nobody in all God's universe who is more orthodox than Satan—he knows all the truth, every bit of it. You can know the truth about yourself, you can know all about the true light, and yet never walk in that true light. The test of a genuine faith in Christ and growth in Christ is submission to Him and growth into His likeness. The evidence that you are truly set free, really saved, really made whole is that you begin to see with the eyes of Christ, you begin to LOVE with the heart of Christ, and you begin to think with the mind of Christ, because Christ is in you, and His character begins to express itself through you. The beauty of Jesus should be seen in you and shine through you. It is all our business here below to cry 'Behold the Lamb . . .', while He must increase and we must decrease.

There is one thing that will characterise the life of every truly born-again believer, and that is love. Love for one another, the desire to care for others, is growth and development. A person who loves will never talk about having already arrived, nor boast in his own righteousness or holiness, nor exalt his own experience of sanctification. There are evidences of his growth in his behaviour. He is more and more filled with the Spirit. He grows more gracious, more gentle and more kind. As clay in the hands of the potter, his life is being moulded and shaped to conform to the image of the Lord Jesus. Someone who has been made fully whole, and is growing up into the stature of Christ's maturity, will have a loving, caring heart, so much so that he will yearn for others to grow also. He will want to share the fullness of his salvation, healing and love, and show others the way to true light, true liberty, and happiness in the Lord.

I want to share with you what Christ has done for me, and is still doing in me. Jesus is able by His almighty power to make a crooked life straight. He is able to make a broken life whole. The life that is marred, sinful, impure, unholy, by the miracle of His grace He can remake into the image of Himself. Isn't that wonderful!

What Christ Has Done for Me

Something really wonderful is happening to me,
I'm growing in the stature of Christ's maturity,
Growing up in grace, and in the knowledge of His word,
My words are polished arrows now, a sharper, swifter
    sword,
The Holy Spirit is revealing deep and wondrous things to
    me,
That fills my heart with vision, and a deeper clarity.

What a wondrous revelation, what a joy to me is this,
Flooding my soul with purest joy and heavenly bliss;
He is opening my eyes and ears, and helps me understand,
The things I could not understand before, the pathway He
    thus planned.
He's enlarging my vision, making things more clear and
    plain,
To why the pathway seemed so weary, and my heart so full
    of pain.

He is healing inner hurts inside me, setting me fully free,
Binding up the wounds and scars that hurt and wounded
    me;
Not only did He save my soul, He's setting painful
    memories free,
He is building up an army, and I know He's chosen me,
Making me a stronger warrior, to run the race for Him,
Giving more power to overcome the tempter, and the sin.

Fulfilled in Christ, victorious, to do His blessed will,
To go where Jesus sends me with a heart that's calm and
    still,
This is the place of perfect rest, and glorious liberty.
Oh yes! it's really wonderful what Christ has done for me,
He is helping me to shut the door on all my yesterdays,
Forgive the wrongs, the cruel abuse, and be Christlike in
    my ways.

To listen—not with just my ears and mind, but in my
    innermost heart,
To give me greater knowledge, and a greater light impart;
My Christian life is brighter now, a clearer light I see,
It's wonderful, it's marvellous, what Christ has done for
    me,
It's growing in me more and more, this sweet and inner
    healing,
Helping me to control my temperament, my hurt and angry
    feeling.

I'm understanding more about myself, the way that I was
    made,
He is giving me more victory, and more courage is
    displayed;
He is shaping me and moulding me, for greater, better,
    newer things,
The way is growing brighter now, through inner healing
    springs;
It's wonderful, it's beautiful what Christ has done for me,
What He's done will last forever, yes for all eternity.

Remember the story of Lazarus in the gospel of John, and how his two sisters Martha and Mary sent for Jesus when he was sick? Remember that Jesus did not come straight away, but told His disciples that the sickness of Lazarus was not the sickness of death, but was instead 'For the glory of God, so that the Son of God might be glorified' (John 11:4)? Then Lazarus got worse and finally died, and they laid him in the tomb. Jesus said plainly, 'Lazarus is dead.' A great stone was laid at the entrance of the tomb, and to all intents and purposes, that was that, or so it seemed to all who knew and loved him.

When Jesus did come—and He always comes, His delay was not a denial—Lazarus had been dead four whole days. Jesus wept when he saw the place where they had laid him, for Jesus knew and loved Lazarus and his two sisters. Real tears ran down the kingly face of Jesus. He entered into their grief and suffering—that's Jesus! He really cares and understands our heartaches. He was the Son of man, as well as the Son of God. Then Jesus commanded those near to Him to roll away the great stone from the entrance of the tomb. Jesus could have moved that stone away with His little finger. He could have commanded the stone to be rolled away, but He said, 'Take ye away the stone' (John 11:39).

There is a great hard stone of doubt, unbelief and confusion set at the entrance of people's hearts today, and Christian, *you* can help roll away the stone. How? With a word of testimony, by the word of authority and power He has given us, and by the power of the Holy Spirit, through whom signs and wonders follow the preaching of the Word of God. There are many ways that we, like Christ's disciples, can help roll stones of doubt and fear away—by a kind and understanding heart filled with compassion and love, by a listening ear, by a smile and a song. This is our work today as His disciples.

When the stone was rolled away, Jesus cried with a loud voice, 'Lazarus, come forth!' (John 11:43) Notice that Jesus called him by his name. It has been said before that if Jesus had not called him by his name, the whole of the dead would have come from their graves. But I like to think that Jesus called him by his name just because He knew him by his name, and loved him by his name. He loves us, and calls us by our name also.

Then Lazarus came forth from the tomb wrapped in grave clothes, and Jesus said, 'Loose him, and let him go' (John 11:44). Jesus did not remove the grave clothes Himself, He told His disciples to do it. It is our job today, as disciples of Jesus, to remove the grave clothes of apathy, fear, unbelief, and every other dark bondage that surround men and women after they come out of the tomb of spiritual death. Even some Christians need grave clothes removed. Some are wrapped in fear, and have grown cold, lacking the power, hope and love they once knew. They have allowed Satan to rob them of victory, peace and joy. Jesus wants us to walk in complete freedom and light, but Satan's job today is to rob Christians of this. If he succeeds, they cannot live truly victorious lives in Christ, because they are still wearing the grave clothes of pride, jealousy, lies, back-biting, and unclean habits, and are restricted in their growth for the Lord.

If we ourselves are wrapped up in grave clothes, covered with fear and doubt, and are in bondage, how can we help others who are bound? We cannot, we need to keep the freedom that Christ has given us before we can do the work that Jesus wants us to do. Jesus wants us to walk and talk with Him, and tell others of His great love. But if we are bound by grave clothes, then our lips are dumb, our hands are bound, our ears are deaf, our eyes are blinded so we cannot see or care about others who are lost. Jesus wants us to grow, to increase in righteousness, wisdom, and power. We are the channels that He wants to use. He is depending on us to do His work—to set captives free, cast out demons, to do exploits in his name, to pull down the strongholds of Satan and to build up His kingdom. 'A true witness delivereth souls' (Prov. 14:25). To love Him is to serve Him, so let us do great things in His name, and go forth in the power of His might into this sin-sick world. Let's go with all His love and power, and reach the lost. The hour is coming when no man can work. Time is short, so let us shake off the grave clothes and work for Him now while we still have the time and opportunity.

God's Instruments

God has no hands but our hands today,
To roll the great stones of hardness away,
We are the finger of God today,
To point souls to Jesus, show them the way,
Out of their bondage and dread of the night,
Out of their darkness into His light.

God has no lips but our lips to speak,
The message of life and love that men seek,
He has no feet but our feet to go—
Just where He leads us, salvation to show,
Jesus has no tongue but our tongue to sing,
The praises of joy to our Saviour and King.

We are the vessels that He wants to use,
To give men the chance to receive or refuse,
The gift of salvation that He longs to give,
To save them from sin, and a new life to live,
Remove all the grave clothes that's binding their soul,
To set captives free, and be made fully whole.

He has given us weapons of warfare to fight,
The whole armour of God, to put Satan to flight,
To come against powers of darkness today,
By the power of His might we can cast them away,
He gives us the strength every battle to win,
He gives us the victory, without and within.

We are His witnesses, and we must stand,
Be ready to reach out and touch someone's hand,
We are the channels from which there can flow,
The life-giving waters wherever we go,
We are the light in this dark world of sin,
So let us burn brightly forever for Him.

I would rather be a doorkeeper in the house of my God, than dwell in the tents of wickedness. We are truly blessed when we dwell in the house of God, and make Him our strong refuge.

I would rather serve the Lord my God than anything else in the world. I would rather be under His almighty sway, than under the sway of Satan and sin. I served the world and the Devil for many long years, and know for a fact that the Devil is a hard taskmaster; but Jesus, my lovely Lord, is a kind and loving Master. It's a great privilege to live and work for Jesus in this world today, no matter how hard the way may seem sometimes. I would rather serve the Lord and be His servant, than be a servant of sin.

I would rather serve His cause than any worldly cause, having my name in lights and receiving the vain applause of men. I would rather dwell in a tent or a tumble-down cottage than live in a grand mansion, in acres of land, with servants and an indoor swimming pool, and all the other luxuries. I would rather have no money in the bank than have a vast sum of wealth and no Saviour, no friend like Jesus. He has a bank of blessing which is overflowing from His Father's throne room in glory. That peace the world can never give, and never take away.

Working for Jesus, living for Jesus, is a joy, and the joy of the Lord is my strength. He alone can give me the grace and strength to carry on, to go where He wants me to go, and to do what He wants me to do. Without Him I can do nothing. He must increase, but I must decrease, and when we put the Lord first in our lives, He will shower His light and love upon us, and our souls will be satisfied.

I would rather do just a little for Jesus, who has done so much for me, than do nothing at all. When we feel weak, then we are strong. Paul said this, and he was right. When we go out in weakness, it is He who gives us the courage to follow where He leads.

I want to sing and shine for Jesus in this dark world of sin, and it's worth it all to see *one* soul saved from the grasp of the Devil. Oh yes! It's worth it all to serve the Lord, and do His will. I would rather follow Him than follow the worldly crowd, and do what man wants me to do.

Sometimes things happen which make it hard to follow Him and do His will. Even people will sometimes try to stop you from serving the Lord with your whole heart. But when you *know* God wants you to work for Him, and has chosen you to work for Him, you will never be happy doing anything else. So let us serve the Lord with gladness. Rejoice in the Lord, and again I say, rejoice!

Oh yes: I would rather serve the Lord, and see His hand touching and transforming lives. Wouldn't you?

Wouldn't You?

I would rather live and work for Jesus—wouldn't you?
And point some other soul to Jesus—wouldn't you?
I'd rather serve His worthy cause, than man's acclaim, and
vain applause,
I'd rather walk the narrow way, with my Saviour day by
day,
By His side I'd rather stay—wouldn't you?
I would rather hear the voice of Jesus—wouldn't you?
And kneel down at His pierced feet—wouldn't you?
I'd rather do His blessed will and all His purposes fulfil,
I'd rather hear my Saviour say—'I'll be with you every day,
I will lead you all the way'—wouldn't you?
I would rather sing the praise of Jesus—wouldn't you?
I'd rather praise my Lord in song—wouldn't you?
Than entertain a worldly crowd, and hear their praises,
false and proud,
I'd rather sing my Saviour's praises loud,
Well, I would—wouldn't you?

Many love songs have been written, beautiful love songs, with words that come straight from the depths of the heart. I often wondered what Jesus really looked like when He was on this earth, walking and talking among men and women. I've often wished I was living then, and had seen Him for myself. But I have seen Him in vision. He looked so kind, so gentle, the love light from His eyes was so pure and beautiful, it cannot be expressed by pen or tongue. Sometimes the vision was clear and sometimes faint, but He was there, He showed Himself to me.

He has spoken to me; and how can I express or explain what His voice sounded like? There is no voice like the voice of Jesus, no voice on the earth—it's rather like the sound of many waters, and sometimes like the musical ring of a rippling spring. He showed me many things, beautiful things, things not of this earth. His voice is plain, it has to be, or we would never understand with our finite minds what He is saying to us.

Sometimes He comes when we are going through a dark valley experience, to encourage us to go on to the light at the end of the seemingly never-ending tunnel. Yes, Jesus comes to us; not always in the same way as He does to others, but He still comes. He longs to come and commune with us, but so often we do not allow Him to—we stop Him from coming right through to reveal Himself to us as He wants to.

God is love, showing Jesus to us, giving Jesus to die for us, to set us free. Jesus is pure love, and if we fully trust Him and let Him take control, He will shine through to us. He is the light of the world, the light of my life, and no matter how much I write about Him and His love, or how much I speak about Him and His love, I could still never, ever, express just how much I love Him. But I have tried to put down on paper a vision I had while I was in prayer, talking to my lovely Lord. As these words were coming to my mind, I knew it was not just from my mind, but from my heart, something I have experienced. No one can rob you of an experience. It's a love song to my Lord, who loved me long before I knew Him.

A Love Song to my Lord

From behind the lattice windows, Jesus shows Himself to
   me,
Faintly through the shadows, I can see Him standing there,
Now His face becoming clearer, misty shadows drift away,
As I softly breathe His Holy name in prayer,
I can see a golden stairway, which leads from earth to
   heaven,
I can hear the voice of my beloved say—
'Lo the winter is now past, the rain is over now and gone,
rise up, my love, my fair one, come away.'

Farewell vain world, I cannot share my lovely Lord with
   you,
My eyes are on my Bridegroom, and it's Him alone I love,
He is altogether lovely, and no other can compare,
So I'm mounting up with wings like a dove,
There's a foretaste now of glory, that one day will never
   end,
His loving arms enfold me, I can hear His voice divine,
I can hear the angels join me, as I sing this sweet refrain—
'I am my beloved's, and my beloved is mine.'

His lips are like the lilies, dropping sweet smelling myrrh,
He is brighter than the morning star, the fairest of the fair,
How beautiful His garden where the beds of spices grow,
Yet He's sweeter than the honey I find there,
He's the blessed Rose of Sharon, and He's blooming in my
   heart,
My song of love for Jesus will never, ever end,
His name is like an ointment, which He pours forth over
   me,
This is my beloved, and this is my friend.

Autumn

Almost everyone is a little sad when summer is over; days get shorter, nights get colder. It's as if another phase of your life is past, as you feel the fresh winds of autumn on your bare arms.

But when you see the beauty of autumn, and its eye-catching, breath-taking splendour, it all seems worthwhile. When you see the hazy sunshine streaking through an avenue of trees, or the vivid scarlet leaves of the maple beside the green conifers that cast long shadows across the still green lawns, it makes your heart sing, especially when you know the Creator of it all.

Nature can teach us many lessons. Jesus Himself used nature to illustrate the parables: the parable of the sower, the parable of the lilies of the field. Jesus said 'He that has ears to hear, let him hear.' If we have the precious gifts of sight and hearing we can open our hearts to everything He wants to teach us, and our eyes will see every beautiful thing on this earth. Nature shows us the goodness of God. He sends rain upon the earth, and rain can speak to us of the blessings which God bestows upon us; whatever they are, they all come from God.

Rain speaks to us of refreshment, cleansing, and growth; if there were no rain, nothing would grow, neither would there be any food. When the rain falls in your life, bringing sorrow and pain to your heart, remember it is all for a reason, and when the rain is over, you can help others along their difficult pathway.

The sun speaks to us of warmth and love. No human being, young or old, can get along without it. Without the sun the crops would never ripen, without the sun there would be no light and no life; we would all die. We can spread some sunshine around, and it does not cost us anything; a smile, a cheery word can help someone who is going through a dark valley, and give them strength and courage to hold on.

Wind also speaks to us. It speaks of change, and in life

there are many changes, just as there are in nature. Change does not come easily to many people, but changes can be good, and often needful, especially after a long illness. A break from the routine of work, and the tensions of everyday living, are very beneficial to us all.

There is another kind of change that is needful—a change of attitude. If people were more prepared to have a change like this, there would be more peace and happiness in the world. A change of heart and mind, a person admitting that he was wrong, has been the start of many reconciliations.

Autumn speaks to us of the ripening grain, the gathering in of the fruits from the fields of toil. It's the time of rejoicing. We can sow seeds; seeds of hope, seeds of love, seeds of faith. Let us sow those seeds, and let us water them. We can sow them in the springtime of our life, while we are still young, we can sow them in the summer of our life, and even in the autumn of our life. We can sow seeds all the time. I would like to encourage those who are young in the Christian faith to sow seeds now—don't leave it until you are older; you can be the means of great blessing and encouragement today. Then when the greatest harvest of all comes, you will have no sad regrets, you will shed no tears of sorrow. We will come rejoicing, bringing our sheaves with us, and our heavenly Father will rejoice to see His seed has grown into good grain.

Autumn Days

In the springtime when the crocuses and daffodils
 appeared,
So many hearts were warmed and glad, so many hearts
 were cheered,
When stately trees awakened from their long winter sleep,
When tiny heads of snowdrops above the ground did peep;
The spring then turned to summer, and all around was seen,
Flowers of red, yellow, and blue, mingling with shades of
 green.

Now autumn days are here again, and yet another change is
 seen,
For leaves on trees and bushes, not long ago so green,
Are changing into scarlet, yellow, brown and gold,
Soon the leaves will tumble down, the evenings will get
 cold.
The farmers and the labourers who work upon the soil,
Are bringing in the harvest from the fields of early toil.

They are gathering in the harvest, the sheaves of golden
 corn,
And store things up for winter, in places dry and warm,
God teaches us from nature how we our lives can live,
We can learn in early days some happiness to give,
By reaching out to those in need, by helping those in pain,
By doing all the good we can, in sunshine and in rain.

Nature always teaches us that God is great and good,
We see this in the sunset, and the flowers in the wood,
If they can show His beauty, His goodness and His light,
Then surely we can do our best to make the world more
 bright;
Always lend a helping hand, and do it with a smile,
Later on we are sure to find that it was all worthwhile.

So sow some seeds of kindness, faith and peace and love,
Reflect the sunlight of God's love that comes from heaven
    above,
Then when our autumn comes along, and we are getting on
    in years,
We will have no sad regrets, no sorrow, and no tears;
And when God sends His angels to take His harvest home,
Great will be rejoicing around the heavenly throne.

Just recently I have been reading through the book of Nehemiah, the man who had a vision, a burden and a commission from God to rebuild the walls of Jerusalem. The walls of Jerusalem were broken down and the gates burned with fire. When Nehemiah heard this he mourned, wept, fasted and prayed before God in heaven. Nehemiah was so sad that it showed on his face, and even the king noticed it and asked, 'Why is thy countenance sad, seeing that you are not sick? This is nothing else but sorrow of heart.' Nehemiah answered, 'Why should *not* my countenance be sad when the city of my fathers' sepulchres lieth waste, the walls broken down and the gates burned with fire?' In other words Nehemiah said, 'I've got every right to look sad when my heart is heavy with grief.'

Today when I myself see the waste places the Devil is making in this land and other lands, the misery, the pain, the wars, the consequences of sin and godlessness, I can understand just how Nehemiah felt. Nehemiah didn't leave it like that, he did something about it. He had a great burden and a great vision, and in the end the king himself commissioned him to go and rebuild the broken walls of Jerusalem.

While his enemies scoffed, Nehemiah prayed to God and continued with the work God had given him to do. It was not an easy task, but Nehemiah never wavered, he just kept on building up the broken walls and gates. He did not do it all alone, the vision caught on to others. In the end he had helpers, and they all got on with the work. Everyone involved had a different but important part to play. The high priest rose early in the morning with his brethren to work, even the women worked (Neh. 3:11).

There was so much to do; much rubbish had to be cleared away so that the building could begin. They were well equipped against the enemy, who conspired to hinder the work right from the very start. While one half worked, the other half held the weapons—spears, bows and shields. Some even worked with *one* hand and held a weapon in the other hand. Some blew with the trumpets to warn of the approaching enemy, these were the watchmen. Each and every worker held a sword girded to his side. They all worked in harmony and unity. How they laboured, from the rising of the sun until the stars appeared at night. How zealous they were in building up the broken walls and gates!

What we need today are men and women like Nehemiah, with a burden and a vision and the courage to get on with building up the waste places the Devil has made and is still making in the sin-sick world we live in. We need to rise up in unity of strength and power to pull down the strongholds of Satan. We need men and women with vision, with courage, with calling and with zeal to do what God wants them to do and to go where God wants them to go. Oh yes, there are scoffers, but you will find that the people who scoff do nothing themselves for the Lord. All they want to do is to tear down, but these are the enemies of God and we have to be vigilant against them—just as the watchmen were in Nehemiah's day.

The Devil is working overtime, diverting and destroying and laying waste precious souls for whom Christ died. We must warn them, we must rescue them before it is too late. We need watchmen who can see with the eye of faith what is needed to build up the kingdom of God. We need more men and women of prayer who can clear away the rubbish that the Devil sometimes blows in at us, like apathy, unbelief, scoffers and those who would discourage us from the work.

The task of God's children is to bring beauty out of ugliness and to create peace where there is discord and strife. God's children, all of us, should be busy creating peace, joy, love and happier relationships wherever we go. We should be telling people about the most important, sweetest relationship of all, that of a personal relationship with the Lord Jesus Christ.

I am glad that I read through Nehemiah. It has helped me. It has enlarged my vision and encouraged me to go on building up the kingdom of God and be a better watchman for Him. The hour is getting very late, the midnight cry goes out today—will you meet the call?

The Midnight Cry

Hark, the midnight cry is sounding, clearer now than e'er
    before,
Behold the Bridegroom cometh, He is even at the door.
Look out on the fields, there is so much to do,
For the harvest is ripe and the labourers are few,
The world is your field and thousands still cry—
For the light of the Gospel—don't leave them to die,
Rise up, trim your lamps, there is no time to sleep,
Look out on the fields, they are ready to reap,
The midnight cry is most urgent and the call we must obey,
How far will we go? every step of the way!
Yes, the way may be hard, we may weep as we sow,
But rejoice as we reap—and for both we must go,
We will rise up to meet Him with sheaves in our hand,
And hear His 'well done' in that great Beulah land.

When I was younger in the faith, and younger in years, I often contacted young women on the streets of Bristol, telling about the love of Jesus.

I will always remember one particular night. I wandered off the main road into a small side street, and almost fell over a group of men, who were half sitting, half lying on the pavement. Newspapers were spread out to offer meagre comfort, and even in the semi-darkness I could see that they were all hopeless alcoholics, the outcasts of society. What a pitiful sight they were. Their eyes were glazed and blank, and their faces bore the marks of sleeping rough and constant inebriation. These men slept where they could, in old derelict houses, bus shelters, or merely by the side of the road. They were constantly moved on by the police. They had nothing to wear but the foul-smelling rags on their backs. They were at the very bottom of society, literally in the gutter.

What had started them on the downward spiral to degradation and hopelessness? What personal tragedies? Broken homes, bereavements, rejection, failure? Whatever the first cause, the enemy of souls had seen to it that their decline led them to the very bottom. Downtrodden miserable forms of humanity—Jesus Christ died for these men. Despite my natural desire to just walk away, because the stench was unbearable, I knew I had to stay and talk to them, for Jesus loved them and He gave His life for all.

I began rather awkwardly, 'Jesus loves you. He can change your lives completely, He can give you joy and peace, and give you a purpose for living.'

They all listened, but whether they understood I did not know. I went on, 'Jesus can chase the dark shadows away, He can set you free.'

As I was talking to them I was praying that Jesus would open their hearts, and break the heavy chains that bound them. I knew nothing short of a miracle could change these men. I asked them their names, but only two of them could remember. I also asked if I could pray for them individually. They were surprised but they agreed. I laid my hand on each man's head, and prayed for the freedom of these prisoners. 'Loose them, Jesus, may they see Thee in all Thy risen power, may they be willing to be free, and find peace in Thee.'

After I had finished praying, the men thanked me most earnestly, and I was deeply moved. I offered to find them shelter, but they weren't interested. Instead they asked me for money. 'I have no money,' I answered truthfully, 'but Christ can give you more than money can buy.'

Suddenly it began to rain, and a wind blew up quite strongly, and the men just got up and disappeared. Once again I was alone in the street. I looked at my watch, and was surprised to find I had been with those men for over an hour. As darkness fell, and despite the rain, people began to come out from behind closed doors, and soon the streets were crowded. Some people were just drifting aimlessly, others hurried along; but they all had the same anxious look, and I continued to contact men and women in this twilight zone. As I walked home, a poem began to take shape in my mind which aptly described my experiences that night. I called it *May they know that somebody cares*.

Later on I wrote another poem, and called it *The story of drunkard Joe*. It is not a true story, but it could easily be true. After all, the Lord can reach everyone, no matter how low they have sunk.

Little did those poor, helpless men know how much encouragement filled my heart after talking and praying with them. My heart was filled with an even deeper love and compassion for lost and sinful mankind. Today let us pray for the homeless. They are not all alcoholics like those men, but they suffer untold heartache and pain. Let us not just forget those who through no fault of their own are homeless, lonely and sad, with no one to care about them. Jesus walks down every street; His eye of love pierces into every dark corner of the world, even the dark streets of the twilight zone.

May They Know That Somebody Cares

I walked the lonely streets tonight,
There was not a single soul in sight,
Yet I knew that every single day,
Lost and lonely people passed along that way,
And all I could do was to pray,
Oh Lord please walk along this street,
Lord Jesus please rest those weary feet,
May they know that somebody cares,
May they know that it is You.

Suddenly I knew that I was right,
For suddenly there burst upon my sight,
A group of homeless people sitting on the ground,
With faces sad and lonely, huddled all around,
And all I could do was to pray,
Oh Lord please walk along this street,
Lord Jesus please rest their weary feet,
May they know that somebody cares,
May they know that it is You.

Suddenly the rain came tumbling down,
And the wind went whistling round the town,
I thought about the people living all around,
Knowing some were lost, knowing some were bound,
And all I could do was to pray,
Oh Lord please walk along this street,
Lord Jesus please rest their weary feet,
May they know that somebody cares
And help me to tell them it is You.

The Story of Drunkard Joe
(Matthew 9:36)

It was dusk in the heart of the city, the air hung damp and
 chill,
For some the day's work had ended, but others were busy
 still.
Some making their weary way homeward, away from the
 bustle and din,
While others were idly seeking the pleasure and folly of sin.
The glitter of lights, the glamour, a laugh, a drink and a
 song,
Rich ladies bedecked in their fine silks and jewels,
With the gay giddy crowd, were fast swept along.

But out on the grimy back-streets, a sad startling
 difference is seen,
Of alleyways dark and narrow, the houses decrepit and
 mean.
Here dwelt the poor and humble, some degraded and
 sunken in shame,
When down the deserted and dimly lit street, a solitary
 figure came.
His garments were torn and tattered, his footsteps
 staggering and slow,
A look of defeat on his sin-stricken face,
Showed the evil of liquor, its curse and its woe.

He lived all alone in a cellar, which was damp and dark and
 low,
Listen awhile, and I'll tell you—the story of drunkard Joe.
For that's what the people called him, as they saw him day
 by day,
With a mocking, scorning finger, as he went along the way.
Pushing his broken-down barrow, all laden with junk and
 rag,
But no-one knew where poor Joe had come from,
Or what kind of up-bringing he had.

One night while alone in the cellar, in his barrow he chanced
to look,
Searching for something to sell for a drink, he found a worn
old book.
Not knowing at first 'twas a Bible, for its leaves were
yellow with age,
Then with shaking, trembling fingers, he turned o'er the
sacred page.
'Though your sins be red as crimson, white as snow they
can be made,
He was wounded for your transgressions, and bruised,
to pardon your iniquities, Christ the debt has paid.'

How memories flooded his being, as he thought of his
mother's face,
Then unchecked tears ran down his face, as he hung his
head in disgrace.
For he came from Godly parents, who had walked the
narrow way,
Who daily read God's Holy Word, and taught him how to
pray.
But led away by evil companions, with the world he had
taken a part,
So drifting further and further away,
He had finally broken his dear mother's heart.

He thought of the old-fashioned mission, where he listened
to words of truth,
And his mind went backward straying, over his wasted
youth.
In gambling dens and pleasure halls, lower he started to
sink,
Deserted by chums when his money was gone and a
helpless slave to drink.
A bottle of liquor for master, for a home, a cold cellar bare,
With only the rats for company at night,
He was lost in the darkness, and deep in despair.

'O can God care for one such as I, after the things I have
    done?'
Then, turning again to the worn old book, he read of the
    Prodigal Son.
A faint ray of hope lit his lonely heart, as he read the story
    of old,
Of how, like Joe, the Prodigal Son had wandered away from
    the fold.
He too had left his father's house into a far country to
    roam,
Until feeding the swine, he had come to himself,
And arose to return to his dear father's home.

The father had seen him coming, and ran out to meet his
    boy,
He fell on his neck and kissed him, filled with compassion
    and joy.
He put a ring on his finger and gave him some shoes to
    wear,
Then he placed the best robe upon him, as repentant he saw
    him there.
While reading that story so tender, there dawned a most
    wondrous light,
Into that darkened cellar and into that sin-sick soul,
Chasing the gloomy shadows away and the awful blackness
    of night.

It was dark in the grimy back-streets, and all was quiet and
    still,
But one was seeking the light of the world, an empty life to
    fill.
For arising from dirt and squalor, still clutching the worn
    old book,
With an air of eager expectancy, Joe the dark cellar
    forsook.
Then coming upon a Mission hall, surrounded by dwellings
    so poor,
And hearing the sound of sweet singing within,
He made no hesitation to go through the door.

And there in the humble Mission hall, blind eyes were made
    to see,
Jesus untied every chain that bound, and set the prisoner
    free.
He bade all demon powers depart and gave such a sweet
    release,
And into Joe's heart and soul that night, there came a
    wonderful peace.
The people wept aloud at the sight of one so torn and
    tossed,
Completely delivered by God's almighty power,
Set free at the foot of the old rugged cross.

As I come to the end of my story, may it bring a message to
    you,
For there's many a soul like drunkard Joe, who's looking
    for happiness too.
May we pray for our souls to be broken, and a burden from
    heaven above,
To follow in Jesus' footsteps, and be moved with
    compassion and love.
For those who are still in the darkness, the devil is out to
    destroy,
To weep and pray for those who are lost,
Then we will doubtless reap with tears of joy.

On the Christian pathway there are times when we have all failed and made mistakes, and we must be honest about it. Not one of us is absolutely perfect, we are not plaster-cast saints but human beings, and as such prone to shortcomings.

There are times when we have all lacked grace, foresight, wisdom, patience, courage and faith, but we must not punish ourselves for it, for Jesus Christ does not punish us. It is the enemy of souls who laughs and says, 'You are nothing but a failure, so give up now.' Instead of lying down in the dust of defeat, we should allow the loving Saviour to pour the oil and wine into our bruised and wounded spirits, and let Him pick us up again. Does God ever get out a big stick and drive us out of the fold because of our shortcomings? A thousand times no! He gently picks us up if we ask Him to, and puts us back on our feet, and encourages us to go forward.

It's not a bit of good staying in the dust, for Satan will only tread us further down. One of his tricks is to tell us we are not good enough, or that we will never rise above our failures. But failures and mistakes bring us to the place of utter dependency on Jesus, the good Shepherd and captain of our souls.

In the Bible we read that some of the greatest men of God failed Him at one time or another. King David was a mighty warrior and a singer of psalms, yet at one time He failed God. But David faced up to his failure, and repented of his sin. We read that David ran into the house of God and caught hold of the horns of the altar and found forgiveness and peace with God.

Peter failed Christ just at the time He needed him most. But Peter repented with tears, he rose above the ashes of denial to lead the church to Pentecost. Even the Apostle Paul wrote in Romans 7, 'What a wretched man I am, who will rescue me?' He goes on to answer, 'Thanks be to God through Jesus Christ the Lord.'

Look upward, not inward, when you fail; cry aloud to God, and He will lift you up, and cause you to rely on the Lord at all times. We cannot come too often to the Lord for help. He won't get fed up with us. That is not His nature at all. He wants us to come to Him.

53

When Peter saw the Lord walking upon the water, He wanted to do the same, and Jesus said to Peter, 'Come'. And Peter walked on the water. But when Peter saw the waves he became afraid, he took his eyes off the Lord, and began to sink beneath the waves. He cried out, 'Lord, save me.' Did the Lord refuse to do so? Of course not! The Lord reached down to Peter with His loving hand and lifted Peter up. He does the same for us when we fail, and take our eyes off the Lord. All we have to do is cry out for help, and help will come.

Although we may fail, Jesus never fails. He remains faithful and true, so this in itself is enough to cause us to praise Him. When we experience such love and tenderness, we will want to worship Him in song. The weakest saint can experience joy, power, release and victory, even when the going gets tough. I like what it says in Isaiah 42:3, 'A bruised reed He will not break, and a smouldering wick He will not snuff out.'

So look up and praise the Lord, rejoice in the Lord, and again I say rejoice.

Deep in My Heart

When I fail and falter on the narrow way,
I cry for help, and hear my Saviour gently say—
'I will lift you up, and help you to go on,'
Deep in my heart He gives a song.

I may not know the skilful use of tongue or pen,
To prove my Lord's redeeming love for sin-sick men,
But this I know, when the path seems hard and long,
Deep in my heart He gives a song.

I may not sing like angels in the choirs above,
But Jesus gave to me a song of joy and love,
I sing because I know that I to Him belong,
Deep in my heart He gives a song.

It's in my heart, this song that Jesus gave to me,
A song of love Divine that sets my spirit free,
When I am weak, my Saviour makes me strong,
Deep in my heart He gives a song.

Winter

It is easy for man to feel that his world is on the verge of collapse, the verge of chaos, out of control, ungoverned, ungovernable; just as the Bible states, men's hearts are failing them for fear over the things that are happening in the world today.

The Devil is busy, he is working overtime in a futile effort to stamp out everything that is good, clean and upright. Even Christians are frequently afraid of him, and avoid talking of him because they find the subject negative and unhappy. By doing so they perpetuate man's historical fear of the Devil, and they fail to help people who are seeking or troubled. In the Bible we can discover the causes of the present evil and discern the pattern of diabolical influence in the world today.

When we open our newspaper or turn on the news, we find sickening accounts of how low man has sunk, horrific accounts of cruelty, rape and murder. It's the sign of the times, the latter times, before Jesus returns to this earth. Spiritual confusion and ignorance overrides man's vaunted knowledge and understanding, and evil continues to get worse, to grow like a weed.

Faced by forces beyond his understanding, modern man is slowly returning to the idea that perhaps there is a Devil after all. Man has come to the awful realisation that behind the evil conditions of this world there must be a power not of this world—a supernatural power. It has been emphasised in popular books and films about the Devil. Fascination with Devil-related themes is big business in Hollywood and the paperback trade. Young people emerge from a movie theatre, where they have just seen a film depicting demon possession, with a mixture of excitement and fear, but hardly an ounce of comprehension. They are made aware of the demonic, without knowing the true way of deliverance and escape from it all—and suddenly they are afraid.

There is an awareness of a Devil and demonic presence,

but it is still beyond the understanding of modern man—worse still, he has little or no assurance regarding the limitation of Satan's power. It pleases Satan when he can strike terror to the human heart, and men and women cower because of the evil he is doing. Misunderstanding, fear, confusion, disorder are all the handiwork of the Devil.

To Christians who read their Bible, there is no fear: 'Perfect love casteth out all fear'. When we read our Bibles we find consolation and reassurance that God is still in control of His universe and His will shall prevail in the end. The Lord is coming soon, and the Devil will be destroyed by the brightness of His coming. The Devil will be banished into the lake of fire. We should not be afraid to warn people about the Devil. We should not be ignorant of the Devil's devices. We can fight the foe and overcome the Devil day by day. Jesus said Himself that evil will increase: 'Look up, for thy redemption draweth nigh'. God's shadow is far greater than any fearful shadow of this day and age, and those who abide beneath the shadow of His almighty wings, need fear no evil at all.

The Day of His Appearing

When we read the daily papers and listen to the news,
Then we read what the Bible has to say
Events we see and read about are foretold in God's Word,
They are signposts to the coming judgment day.
We are living in the latter times, there's trouble
  everywhere,
With earthquakes, false prophets, division and war,
Men's hearts are failing them for fear on every hand,
As wickedness increases more and more.

Evil signs and lying wonders and scoffers all around,
Blasphemers, who God's holy Word deny,
Dark powers will soon be shaken, sun and moon will cease
  to shine,
All the stars will be falling from the sky.
Then a far greater light will be seen in this dark world,
When the Son of Man in power and glory comes,
With a host of holy angels in a radiancy so bright,
It will outshine a thousand, million suns.

There is no condemnation for the blood-bought child of
  God,
No fear of punishment, no death, no pain,
We are looking for that blessed hope, when Jesus we will
  see,
Then forever with our Saviour we shall reign.
For we shall be changed in a twinkling of an eye,
When we rise up to meet Him in the air,
Receive a crown of glory that fadeth not away,
In the city of our God bright and fair.

As in the days of Noah, before the mighty flood,
Man continues in rebellion just the same,
All those outside the ark of salvation will be lost,
Very soon the Lord will shut the door again.

So let us be as watchmen, and warn them of the night,
Let us raise up our banner, hold it high,
Lift up our voice like a trumpet—shout aloud,
The coming of the Lord is drawing nigh.

Watch therefore, for ye know not what hour your Lord doth come. (Matt. 24:42)

Under His Wings
(Psalm 91)

Underneath the shadow of His mighty wings,
Music sweetly flows from healing fountain springs,
Soothing all my worry, like a lullaby—
That a mother sings to hush her baby's cry;
Neath His downy feathers, I will lay my head,
Fearing no destruction, or the plagues of dread,
Dwelling in the secret place of my Lord most high,
Nothing here can harm me, knowing He is nigh.

Resting, still and quiet, in this place of peace,
Where from earth's great flurry, storms and tempests cease,
No evil can befall me, He doth guard my soul,
Everything is safely under His control;
Snare of the fowler, terror of the night,
Arrows of the daytime, all are put to flight,
With truth my shield and buckler, my refuge He will be,
In this blest habitation, He will deliver me.

Thousands fall around me, my feet will firmly stand,
For angels bear me upwards, with their heavenly hand,
Dragon, lion and adder, I will trample down,
He set His love upon me, like a glorious crown;
When I call upon Him, He will answer me,
In the time of trouble, He will set me free,
He heals the hurts inside me, oh the joy it brings,
Resting in the shadow of His mighty, holy wings.

Not many of us are willing to humble ourselves. If however, external events turn against us, failure, disgrace or great physical pain may force it on us. When this happens we must take advantage of it; it can teach us many lessons.

I myself have experienced suffering in mind, body and soul, and therefore in some measure I can understand and try to help those who suffer and go through great darkness. If we ourselves do not suffer, how can we fully help those who are suffering?

Suffering brings meekness. This is a key which opens the door to prayer. The meek and humble in spirit find it easier to pray, not just for themselves, but for others who suffer and need our prayers. Jesus suffered and went through test after test, and there is nothing the He does not see or care about. He was despised and rejected of men, a man of sorrows and acquainted with grief.

Jesus really does care about what we suffer, His eye of love pierces into every dark corner of this globe. Our blessed Lord walked this earth before us, and He had to experience what every man experiences. He knew pain and suffering, hunger and thirst, loneliness. He was willing to go through so much for us, because He loved us so much.

We as His disciples should be prepared to follow in His footsteps, follow just where He leads, even through the dark valley. This is where we come to grips with grief and pain and often humiliation. Every test, every valley experience, is for a divine purpose, there are great lessons we can learn through trials and testings that would otherwise never be learnt at all. We may not be aware of it, but a most beautiful work is being wrought in our souls by the Lord Jesus Himself. We can come through great darkness, into the sunshine, with more faith, more grace, more patience and understanding, more assurance and confidence than ever before.

I had a most wonderful vision when going through a very trying and difficult time in my life—it was a vision of jewels. The walls of clay, the sin and shame had been broken down, and I was surrounded by thick walls of jewels. There were rubies, pearls, sapphires, emeralds and diamonds, and each jewel meant something. The red rubies meant the fire of His Holy Spirit, His love for me, my love for Him, His work, and my zeal for souls. The blue sapphires stood for loyalty—the Lord's faithfulness to me, and mine to Him. The pure white stones stood for purity, light, conviction. Each jewel was given to me by Jesus Himself. I was smothered in them, and what a wonderful sight it all was.

I was rich, rich in His love and mercy. Jesus spoke to me and said, 'Store up these jewels to help you in the dark days ahead and scatter these jewels around to people who are poor in spirit.' So I began to scatter around these beautiful jewels. Some people caught them. Some caught them and just dropped them, and some were trampling the pearls under their feet. This grieved me, and so I said, 'Look Jesus, they are trampling the precious jewels under their feet, so shall I stop scattering them around?' 'No,' said Jesus, 'you go on scattering them, some will catch them.' I learned a lesson through this vision—we can come up through the darkness with treasure that money cannot buy. It can be a treasure we can share, or we can come up from the darkness with a cold, bitter heart which will not help anyone. So this poem comes from my own personal experience. Each time I have come through deep, dark experiences, I come up richer for it—so let me share the jewels with you. Catch them, they are *free*!

Treasures of Darkness

Miners go right down underground,
To dark and gloomy places,
Digging up coal to keep us warm,
With dusty hands and faces,
'Black gold' they sometimes call it,
For it glitters and burns like gold,
To warm our human hands and hearts,
In the winter's wind and cold.

Others dig for rarer jewels,
Real gold, and diamonds that shine,
But they would never bring any treasure up,
If they did not first go down the mine;
When you travel into the darkness,
Remember that while you are there,
You can dig from the wealth of experience,
And bring up some treasure rare.

There's the rare jewel of patience,
That I found at pain's dark door,
And the shining jewel of hopes bright ray,
That I could not find before;
There are radiant gems of faith and love,
That will shine out to all around,
If you did not go into the darkness,
These treasures might never be found.

In the long dark watches of the night,
When you cannot, and do not sleep,
He will give you the treasures of darkness,
And these you will always keep,
You can store up these jewels for life's winter days,
Keeping faith's walls firm and stout,
From the sudden storms of discouragement,
And the cold winds of bitterness out.

There is treasure in secret places,
In the secret places of prayer,
You can find many jewels in God's Holy Word,
And these you will want to share;
So scatter around some sparkling jewels,
There are plenty in God's treasure store,
Dig deep and you will find them,
Then they're yours for evermore.

In Hebrews 4:9 we read, 'There remaineth therefore a rest to the people of God.'

Rest does not imply laziness or inactivity. It is movement without friction, creating harmony and peace. It also means balance, which results from every part of our lives being centred in the will of God. We are enriched by Him, not of ourselves or by our own works, all things are imparted to us by His grace and love. We can know perfect rest and peace in trusting Christ and complete trust can only come by constant growth and constant surrender to Him day by day, hour by hour.

We need not spend sleepless nights fretting and worrying if we are completely surrendered to Him. We can know without one shadow of a doubt that He is in absolute control of every situation. Fretting or worrying will not change anything and will not change the course He has set for us to run. We can run the race with rest and confidence, peace and love, knowing everything is safely in His hands. His hands are strong, and His words are true. There *is* rest for the people of God, if they rest in Him.

Sometimes the Lord has woken me up from my sleep, but it has always been for a purpose. The wind has been howling, the rain lashing down, but I have not been afraid even though I have sometimes been going through a trial. Trying times need not make us restless and afraid when we know that it is He who has allowed it and we still trust Him to see us through. Very often the Lord has woken me up to pray; most of my writing has been done in the middle of the night when the rest of the family has been fast asleep. There has been a heavenly hush in my study, despite the howling winds and noise outside. There has been a perfect stillness in my heart and soul, proving the fact that He never slumbers or sleeps, and is watching over us every single hour of the day and night.

We live in a very sinful, very restless and wicked world. A lot of wickedness is done in the middle of the night. Having once been in the grip of Satan's power as a witch and satanist, I know what wickedness goes on in the night, and not only in the night, but in the day time also. I have proved that the Lord Jesus protects His own, for He has protected me. The Psalmist says in Psalm 91:5—6 'Thou shalt not be afraid for the terror by night; nor for the arrow that flieth by day, nor for the pestilence that walketh in darkness; nor for the destruction that wasteth at noonday.' I have proved this Psalm time and time again. One night while I was praying, I actually heard the sound of the Lord's wings hovering over me. His feathers made a sweet swooshing sound, a hushing sound, a soothing sound. It was so beautiful no words can describe it. His wings were protecting me, engulfing me, all was still, the wind ceased from howling, and all I could hear was the sound of His wings, and with the eye of faith I could see how beautiful and how big they were.

After this experience I was prompted by the inspiration of the Holy Spirit to write the next two poems. I trust they will be a great blessing to those who read them. Yes, the world may be a very restless, sinful world, and dark things go on in the night, but the child of God can know perfect rest and peace. Those dark things need not harm him or make him afraid. The blood of Jesus is also covering, so with His feathers, His wings and His precious blood—why need we be afraid? Remember His shadow is far greater than any fearful shadow of the night. One wonderful day the Lord will return to reign upon this earth, and there will be no more wickedness, all sorrow and sinning will cease; but until that time comes, we can rest underneath the shadow of His almighty wings. He will keep us safe in the hollow of His hand. Enter now into His rest. He will not fail you—there's nothing to fear.

Anchored in Jesus

Though dark clouds may gather, and fierce storms arise,
When the tempest is raging—then lift up your eyes,
Jesus, your pilot, your pathway has planned,
And nothing can pluck you out of His hand.
You're anchored in Jesus, firm and secure,
He'll guide your vessel safe to the shore.

Though dark be the valley, and strong be the winds,
You're sheltered and safe, 'neath His almighty wings,
Jesus, your captain, is still in control,
Nothing can harm you, He keepeth your soul;
His hands on the rudder, there's nothing to fear,
You're anchored in Jesus, so be of good cheer.

I Understand Your Sorrows

Do not let your heart be troubled,
Neither let it be afraid at all,
In Jesus there's no darkness,
The night is like the day,
You will hear His voice softly say—
'I understand your sorrows my child,
I'll wipe away each falling tear,
Oh come to me, Oh trust in me,
My perfect love will cast out every fear.'

He will never leave you or forsake you,
He's with you every moment of the day,
His love is strong and faithful,
His voice is sweet and true,
This is what He says to you—
'I understand your sorrows my child,
I'll wipe away each falling tear,
Oh come to me, Oh trust in me,
My perfect love will cast out every fear.'

'I am your Shepherd, I will lead you,
If you just simply follow me each day,
Trust in me, lean on my arms,
I will never let you go,
My life and love forever you will know;
I understand your sorrows my child,
I'll wipe away each falling tear,
Oh come to me, Oh trust in me,
My perfect love will cast every fear.'

Through every long, dark lonely night, through every pain-filled day, when everything goes wrong, in every agonising decision, in bitter disappointments, through all the hurts that life brings along, in good times and in bad—I've learned something, and I'm still learning. I am learning to trust.

Life is a process of learning. Life is a school of learning where we never take a final exam and qualify. We can never say, 'I know it all, there is nothing more to learn.' I've learned something through the past days. Some were exhausting and demanding days, others exciting and bright days. But in all of them I have been learning to trust my Lord.

Sometimes we have to unlearn things, things which we have so rigidly clung to, which we thought were right and good but in the end brought us into bondage. The good things long forgotten have to be relearned, and new things, better things, have been added to those things already learned.

I'm learning to trust. Trust—what a word that is! Babies are born with it, little children have it in abundance, but adults, wayward and disillusioned (as we often are with all our preconceived ideas) must learn to trust.

If everything was easy, every pathway clear, if there were no darkness, no pain, no difficult and trying days, where and how could we learn to trust? Jesus, who walked this way before us, knows every trial, every heartache, every temptation. He wants us to walk with Him, trusting Him through the dark shadows as well as in the sunshine. When things go wrong, when faith seems to get up and run away, when storm clouds gather, it is then that Jesus sweetly whispers, 'Come unto me, trust me.' Did He fail me then? Will He fail me now? He cannot fail!

When the sudden hurts of life shock us, and we just cannot undrstand the reason why something has happened to us, when with trembling lips and tear-filled eyes we have cried out, '*Why?*' Did He hear us then? Did He not undertake for us, and lift us up and help us to go on? Jesus was praying for us then and He is praying for us right now, so I am learning to trust Him through it all. I am depending on Him to see me through each fiery trial, because He has been with me, and helped me in the past, so I know He will be with me to help me in future days, no matter what they may bring.

Jesus fills me with wonder because of His mighty, tender, humble dealings with me. He is my friend, my reliable, faithful friend. He still loves me despite my failure to trust Him when I should have done. When I have vainly tried to work things out for myself, when I have tried and failed to unravel the tangled threads of confusion and fear that have filled my heart and mind. Did He leave me then? Will He leave me now? He cannot fail me! His nature decrees it, His word declares it, His love displays it; our God reigns and He cannot fail.

He loved me enough to die for me. He loved me enough to turn me around, to change me from the person I once was, to the person I am today. He gave me everything I have today—my home, my children, my love for Him, and my love for every lovely thing on this earth. The courage to comfort, the discernment to see and know what is needed and how to give it. The patience to listen, the strength for each daily task. It all comes from Him because He loves me so much, so I am learning to trust Him more and more.

I am learning to respond with confidence to His love, to have faith in His ability to lead me through each new trial, knowing that He is in absolute control of every situation, to realise that there are many valuable lessons to be learned from each one, and that there is always something to be thankful for.

There are so many others who suffer the same heartaches, the same pain as I do, yet they suffer so much more because they do not know the Saviour, therefore they have never learned to trust Him. So I must learn to trust Him through every dark period of my life, in order to point them to Jesus Christ so that they may trust Him also. When the pressures of life have left them utterly exhausted, broken and so desperately lost with nowhere and no one to turn to, I can say with full assurance and full confidence, 'God is love, He understands and cares.' Because I have learned to trust myself.

Life is not always what we want, or what we expect. Life has its disappointments and hurts, that's unavoidable. But we can learn to trust Him to bring us through these times. How we respond to the things which try our faith, to the things which God allows to happen in our lives, really matters. To respond with anger and resentment brings more hard problems and saddens His heart. We must all learn to respond in complete confidence in Him, knowing that His ways are best for us, and that there is a divine purpose in each one of them.

All my tomorrows are in His strong, capable hands. He is in full control of my life and my future pathways. My bruised heart will heal again, my fears will be dispelled. All my sighings will turn to singing yet again. My tears (for tears will come) will change to smiles once more. My losses will turn out best for me. I am learning from experience to lean harder on my Lord. I am learning to trust, to have faith in, and to stand upon His Word. This is my map, my lesson book in the school of life and for each lesson of faith until term is over and I see His lovely face. Then I shall know, more than ever I have known, that it was worth it all put my trust in Him.

Learning to Trust
(Proverbs 3:5)

Life is a school of learning, and I am learning something
    new—
That in every situation, my Lord will see me through.
Demanding days, exhausting days, when everything goes
    wrong,
In bitter disappointments, when my heart seems void of
    song.
I am learning to trust my Saviour more, to know that He is
    there,
To lift me up and strengthen me, for every cross I bear,
In all the hurts life brings along, to dry each falling tear,
To draw me closer to Him, and whisper, 'Do not fear.'

I am learning to have faith in God, to know His ways are
    best,
Learning to stand upon His Word, and on His promise rest.
His Holy Word, my lesson book, my atlas and my guide,
The Holy Spirit teaches me, and never leaves my side.
He teaches me to praise the Lord in good times and in bad,
When my heart is glad and happy, and when my heart is sad,
On bright days, exciting days, when not a cloud's in sight,
In dark days and dreary days, when skies look black as
    night.

When I have vainly tried, and failed, to work my problems
    out,
Instead of trusting Jesus have been filled with fear and
    doubt—
Did Jesus fail or leave me then, or cast my soul away?
His word declares He cannot fail, He's faithful all the way.
He gave me everything I have, my love for every lovely
    thing,
My peace, my joy, my hope, my love, I owe it all to Him.
So all my unknown pathways, with all their unknown plans,
All my unknown tomorrows I am leaving in His hands.

I am learning to respond with faith, with confidence and
    grace,
I know that He will help me stay the course, and run the
    race.
I am learning not to question, or ask the reason why,
I know that I will understand in heaven, bye and bye.
When the school of life is over, and all battles fought and
    won,
I will look upon His lovely face, and hear His glad, 'Well
    done.'
Then I'll know that it was worth it all, to trust the
    Saviour's love,
When I reign with Him eternally, in His bright home above.

In Philippians 2:7 we read, 'He made Himself of no reputation, and took upon Himself the form of a servant, and was made in the likeness of man.' Again in John 13:4 we read, 'He riseth from supper and *laid aside his garments* . . .' This speaks to us of Jesus laying aside all the glory, all the splendour He had with His Father, before the world began. He willingly laid it aside to come down to this dark world of sin. He chose a lowly cattle shed to be born in. He could have chosen a grand mansion, or a palace, but instead He chose a cattle shed. He surrounded Himself with humility and the lowly things, the things pertaining to man. That's Jesus!

He chose a lowly, unknown Jewish maiden for an earthly mother, and a carpenter for an earthly father. He took an ass's colt to ride upon. He took little children up into His arms and He blessed them. That's Jesus—that's the one I love and serve today. He blessed with His kind word, His kind look, His healing hands. He blessed bread for the multitudes. Everywhere He went He was a blessing.

What a blessing it was for that poor widow woman who lost her only son, when Jesus placed His loving hands upon that coffin and said, 'Young man, arise.' Then He gave him back to his mother. What joy, what blessing! What a blessing it was for that poor blind man, who had never seen his mother's face, never seen the light of day, when Jesus touched those blind eyes, and he received his sight. What blessing! What a blessing it must have been for that poor leper—he had no friends, no home, and no hope. He earned his living, like the blind man, begging by the wayside. He was a hideous, repulsive sight to the passer-by. Everyone avoided him; yet Jesus actually touched those ugly leprous sores, and he was instantly made whole and clean. What a wonderful blessing! What a blessing it was for that man who dwelt among the tombs and was always cutting himself with stones. No man could tame him. They often tried to chain him up, but the demon powers were so strong that he just plucked them off just as though they were paper chains. When Jesus cast out the legion of demons and he was free, he sat clothed and in his right mind at the feet of Jesus. What a tremendous blessing!

77

Jesus is the same today. He still blesses us. He still touches us if we will let Him. He blesses us when we gather in His name to worship Him and when we speak to Him in prayer. He blesses us when we gather around His table to partake of the bread and wine and remember Him. He blesses us all the time, He cannot do otherwise. He loves us so much and He longs to pour out His blessing upon us, but so many of His children stand on the very threshold of blessing and never receive it. Through fear, doubt and other hindrances they go so far and no further. What a great pity!

Jesus wept. He broke into tears over sinful, wayward Jerusalem, and said, 'How oft would I have gathered you beneath my wings, as a hen would gather her young, but ye would not.' Jesus wept when He saw dead Lazarus in the place where they had laid him. When He saw Mary and Martha, his sisters weeping, and the Jews weeping, we read, 'Jesus wept'. He entered into their suffering. That's Jesus! What a wonderful Saviour! Yet out of the many thousands who lived on this earth when Jesus lived among men, only a few wanted Him. 'He came unto His own, and His own received Him not.' Out of the thousands that live on this earth today, only a few really want Jesus; the rest will not receive Him, they do not want any change in their lives. What a pity! If only they knew what Jesus could mean to them and what He could do for them. All they need is just one glimpse of Jesus, and how different their lives would be.

One day they crucified this lovely Jesus who did so much good. They led Him away to the dark hill of Calvary outside the city wall, and they put Him to death. He gave and gave while He was here on the earth, until finally He gave Himself as a ransom for many. He gave Himself so that we might go free through the shedding of His own precious blood. The whole world might be saved if they came to Him —for forgiveness, light and freedom from darkness and sin.

And Jesus arose from the dark cold tomb of death, victorious over the grave. And He is *still alive today*. He is still healing the sick, still transforming hearts and lives, still touching, still blessing, and still delivering from the power of the devil. What a Saviour! All we have to do is come to Him, take the first step toward Him, and He will do the rest. He will take the heavy burden of sin away, all the pain, all the heartaches and all the fears. He will wash us clean, make us whole and make us a blessing in this world. Make room for this loving, gentle Saviour in your life today. You will never regret it.

Give Him Our Everything

Down from the glory in heaven He came,
Down to this dark world of sin,
Born in a manger, rude and bare,
For there was no room at the inn,
No room for the Saviour, God's well beloved son,
Humbly and lowly His life begun.

Tempted in all points, and yet without sin,
Obedient in doing His Father's will,
Blessing small children, healing the sick,
Bidding the wind and the waves to be still,
Down to the lowest His arm would extend,
Declaring Himself the sinner's friend.

They led Him away to the judgment hall,
There to be mocked and tried,
They cruelly scourged and spat upon Him,
Then led Him away to be crucified,
Lowly His thorn-crowned brow was bent,
Bearing for us the punishment.

But He rose up again from the cold, dark tomb,
Conquering death and the grave,
The dear loving Saviour is living today,
Still mighty and strong to save,
Worthy the Lamb to be praised and adored,
Risen, ascended, our glorious Lord.

His birth, life and death, His rising again,
Made for us a new living way,
So let us make room in our hearts and lives,
For the dear Son of God today,
Let us worship again the heavenly King,
And give Him our everything.

We are living in very troubled times. Everywhere you go, you can see sadness and pain and people with enormous problems. There are so many broken-hearted people living in the world today. I have often wished I could solve all the problems, mend all the broken hearts, but I know I cannot do that. The Lord has told me time and time again, 'Do what you can, and leave the rest to me.'

People are living under terrific pressure today. It shows on their faces. People on trains, on buses, in the busy streets, in shops and offices all look worried. We cannot all go around with a perpetual grin on our faces—this would be false—but I for one don't want to look as if I carried the whole world on my shoulders.

It's rush, rush, rush today, and many do not know what it's like to rest and enjoy the world God has made. The bondage of care and anxiety, fear and uncertainty can be so heavy that it completely blocks out the beauty of creation: the peaceful countryside with the winding, rippling brook running through the leafy glade—the tiny flowers, the song birds on the wing, the tall trees gently swaying in the summer breeze.

People fear evil, and this affects them in their everyday life. Although evil abounds, we must not fear it and constantly speak about it. This is fatal to the love and peace God bestows upon us. Some Christians have mistakenly thought that because I was once a witch, and practised evil, I would be speaking constantly about dark, evil things—how little they know me. Although I expose evil when I am required to, so that Christians are not ignorant of the Devil's devices, I am not *always* speaking about the Devil. In fact, I am far happier when I am preaching the gospel story without even mentioning my past life.

I love to express all the beautiful things around me. I love to paint in oils and write poetry about the goodness and love of God. I love gardening and tending flowers. I love to ponder the goodness of God and the great and lovely things that are happening in the world. Good things are still happening. Kind and loving people still exist, despite the evil and wrong.

I believe we are truly sanctified when we can live in this busy, restless world, amid all the wrong, with hope and light in our hearts, radiating the beauty of Jesus Christ in all we say, reflecting His love and grace to those who are lost. I want to spread some sunshine around, the sunshine of His love, the sunshine of His smile, bringing glad tidings, revealing positive faith, positive thinking and believing. My Lord is a positive Lord, and with Him as my Shepherd I will fear *no* evil, for in Him there is no darkness at all.

Think on These Things
(Philippians 4:8)

There is so much that is evil in this world today,
All the while, new headlines it is making,
So we cannot ignore it, it's there all the time,
There are so many hearts that are breaking.

If we constantly dwell on the wrongs of this world,
The things that are ugly and bad,
It will bring us right down to the depths of despair,
And make our hearts heavy and sad.

So think of the beautiful things in the world,
Things honest and pure and good,
Lovely thoughts, kindly deeds and loving, tender care,
Still flourish and grow, like the flowers in the wood.

We still see glorious blossoms in the spring time,
The splendour of the setting summer sun,
The clean sweet perfume of the soft dewy rose,
All speak of good God has done.

So let what we say be of good report,
Restoration, and healing it brings,
If there be any virtue, if there be any praise,
Let us then think on these things.

Winter Glory

I have shared with you the joys and delight of springtime, summer and autumn. Now we are in the depths of winter. How quickly time passes. Now, dear reader, let me take you by the hand once again, and let us wander through the charms of winterland. We leave the warmth and comfort of the thatched cottage, with its open log fire, which sends flickering shadows across the oak-beamed ceiling, and we venture out into the cold, crisp winter air, with Sandy, the golden Labrador at our heels.

There has been a sharp frost, which has given the green grass a coat of white spikes, which crunch beneath our feet as we set out on our winter walk. Winter is indeed here, it is very cold, but we are well wrapped up with brightly coloured woollen hats, scarves and gloves, which add warmth to the winter scene. The sky above is mostly grey, but slightly streaked with a silver light on the horizon; maybe we shall have some sunshine later on. There is no wind, all is strangely hushed and still, as if all nature were asleep, yet poised, ready to awaken at any moment. As we enter the woods, we suddenly hear the flurry of wings, and we lift our eyes to see a blackbird rise with effortless grace from the tall bare trees, whose twisted branches blend into beautiful patterns against the grey sky. How very lovely it is, and how good God is to give us such a variety of beauty with each season. Winter has a beauty all its own.

We let Sandy off the lead now, and he scampers off ahead of us eager for some adventure; his golden coat stands out as he weaves his way through the thicket. Just before we leave the short footpath through the wood, a rabbit, with a flash of its white tail runs across the path ahead of us, and disappears into the thick undergrowth. Sandy spots it and gives chase with excited barking; picking up the scent he sniffs around, and is reluctant to give up the search, and at first ignores us when we call him. He finally gives up, and bounds towards us, his tail wagging with glee; he certainly enjoyed the challenge.

We leave the footpath, and turn onto the road which wends its way downhill towards the sea. The gardens, which just a few months ago were ablaze with colourful annuals, and alive with the activity of butterflies and bees, now give an air of quiet dignity and repose. This reminds us of the words in Ecclesiastes 3:1, 'There is a time for everything, and a season for every activity under heaven.' There is a time for us to rest from our labours, we must allow time in our lives to relax and enjoy ourselves. Many people are busy doing things, and do not allow time for relaxation. God wants us to relax and enjoy the gifts He has given to us—our partners, our children, our parents, our homes, our gardens, our world.

The evergreens stand out with greater beauty now winter is here. This speaks to us of faithfulness. Sometimes we need to be reminded of faithfulness, for faithfulness can be taken for granted. So let us remember and be grateful, and appreciate faithfulness whenever we see it. The faithfulness, and steadfast love of our Heavenly Father never ceases, His mercies never come to an end, they are new every morning.

Not everything has faded, in fact there is much to see in winter, things which are often missed at other seasons. Variegated ivy and evergreen rock plants cascade over stone walls; beneath the sturdy laurel, sheltered from the frost, the cyclamen is still in flower, with its pretty pink heads peeping up from heartshaped leaves. What a glorious sight. The holly bushes are laden with bright red berries; no doubt some will be brought inside for decoration, reminding us that Christmas is only a few weeks away. Already Christmas trees are in the windows, aglow with twinkling lights, tinsel, and gold and silver bells, which bring joy and cheer to every passer-by. It's the season of good will, it's the season of rejoicing that the Saviour came to the earth as a babe, born in a stable, and lived among men, to bring everlasting life and peace to all who receive Him.

Passing the houses and gardens we have now reached the sea, who now has the shore all to herself. The tide is coming in, and the waves, with a soft murmur, gently lap onto the brown sand. Cliffs, tall and majestic, tower above the sea on either side, almost as if they were protecting her, enfolding her with their strength against the rigor of winter. We also know strength and protection at all times, for we read in Psalm 27:5, 'For in the day of trouble He will keep me safe in His dwelling, He will hide me in the shelter of His tabernacle and set me high upon a rock'. How good it is to know our Father's loving arms enfold us, keeping us safe in the time of storm, for He is our rock and our fortress.

It is now late afternoon, the sky has lost its silver light, the sun did not shine after all, and the clouds are now low and heavy with snow. Our hearts are not heavy, for the promise of sunshine is there, the sun will shine again, even in the winter months. Later on, in the spring, the trees and bushes which are asleep, will wake up and burst into new buds, new leaf and blossom will appear, the warmth of the spring sunshine will herald the arrival of hosts of beautiful flowers for us to enjoy.

There are those living around us whose lives are bleak and empty, and we, by showing warmth and love, patience and understanding, gentleness and goodness, peace, faith and joy—things which come only from God—can enable them to find 'new birth' in the warmth of God's love.

As we leave the sea, and start to climb the hilly road, which runs parallel to the road we came down, it begins to snow. Soft white snowflakes are falling thick and fast; they melt on our warm faces, but begin to lie on the dry hard ground. Snow has come early; 'I wonder if we will have a white Christmas?' we both say together; our thoughts are the same. Sandy, who has never seen snow before, snaps playfully at the flakes as they fall, and snorts and sniffs at the snow on the ground, making us laugh.

Our footsteps quicken as the snow falls thick and fast, we can hardly see the way ahead. We are conscious of bright flashing Christmas lights from the windows on either side of us. Finally we reach the top of the hill, and here we pause to catch our breath. Suddenly it stops snowing, and we gaze in wonderment at the scenery all around us. Everything is clothed with a pure white coat of snow, transforming the landscape into a winter wonderland. Lights from the houses nestling in the valley below give the snow a golden gleam, and all is hushed and still. So winter richly unfolds her splendour and lays it on the altar of mankind; how privileged we are to behold it, and what a pleasure it is to receive it. The snow reminds us of those wonderful words in Isaiah 1:18, 'Come, let us reason together says the Lord. Though your sins are like scarlet, they shall be as white as snow; though they are red as crimson, they shall be like wool.' The blood of Jesus shed on Calvary's cross covers all our sin, His blood blots our past out when we receive Him as our Saviour. Just as He clothes the hillside with snow in winter, so He clothes us with garments of pure white, the robes of righteousness.

Just as we turn the corner we see to our delight a robin sitting on a gate, his red breast stands out boldly against the soft white snow. It puts the finishing touch to the picture; everything we have seen on this memorable walk has been just like a picture on a Christmas card; yet it is real, we have seen it with our own eyes. Now we see the welcoming lights from the cottage just ahead of us; we are nearly home. Nearly home! Does that strike a chord of longing in your heart? On our earthly journey we are just pilgrims, there are paths before us that we have not trod, but let us take heart, for there is one who walks before us, He is our light, and He will safely guide our footsteps to our heavenly home. There is a light on the shore that will guide us into the heavenly harbour, so be of good cheer.

The smoke from the chimney curls lazily into the grey sky, which tells us that a warm fire awaits us. How good to know someone is waiting for us to return, let us appreciate that. So many would dearly love to know and experience a happy home, with someone to welcome them. Sandy shakes his golden coat as we enter, and someone says, 'Welcome back, did you have a nice walk?' I leave you to answer that, I know I did. There is a hot drink, some sandwiches and mince pies for us, and we tuck in gratefully, our walk certainly gave us an appetite.

The Christmas tree has arrived, and there are trimmings scattered around, and Christmas wrapping paper, soon the tree will be decorated and gifts will be placed under the tree. Yes! Christmas is nearly here, the spirit of Christmas is with us already. May this spirit of goodwill, gladness and love remain with us forever, for that's how God wants it to be. As we give and receive gifts at this season, let us remember the greatest gift of all, the gift of God's Son, the Lord Jesus Christ, who came to this world that we might have the gift of eternal life.

The year is drawing to a close, we have journeyed through all the seasons together, and now, dear reader, I say farewell. We may meet in person one day. If not, I pray that it will be in the time 'When the redeemed of the Lord shall return and come with singing unto Zion; and everlasting joy shall be upon their heads; and sorrow and mourning shall flee away.' For then we shall be at home with the Lord.

A Happy New Year in Jesus

As we come to the end of another year
We can look back, and truthfully say,
It's been wonderful walking with Jesus,
Trusting Him day by day,
Yes! there may have been times of testing,
Days of darkness, sorrow and pain,
But He gave us new grace for each trial,
He has blessed us again and again,
He has blessed with His peace and protection,
He has chased away darkness and fear,
He has blessed with the power of His presence,
He has guided us all through the year.

So a happy New Year in Jesus,
New blessings He's waiting to give,
New love for the lost, new light from His word,
That those in the darkness might live.
He can show us new pathways of service,
He can give us new power in prayer,
Fresh vision, new purpose, more courage and faith,
New joy of salvation to share.
Greater love for our brothers and sisters in Christ,
Deeper wisdom, new kindness and grace,
More ready and willing to comfort and bless,
More patience to run the race.

A happy New Year in Jesus our Lord;
This is my heart's prayer for you,
May your pathway be filled with new blessings,
For this is what Jesus wants too.
May the light of His love shine upon you,
Your strength and your joys to increase,
Flood your heart and life with His glory and praise,
And grant you His sweet, perfect peace,
So commit each new day to the Saviour,
Trust Him, and be of good cheer,
Put your hand in the hand of the Master,
Then it *will* be a happy New Year.